Paddle Steamers of Australia

P.S. Canberra - The First Hundred Years

Published by Brolga Publishing Pty Ltd
ABN 46 063 962 443
PO Box 12544
A'Beckett St
Melbourne, VIC, 8006
Australia

email: markzocchi@brolgapublishing.com.au

National Library of Australia Cataloguing-in-Publication entry
Author: Conner, Beth, author.
Title: Paddle steamers of Australia : P.S. Canberra - The First Hundred Years/
           Beth Conner & Peter Garfield.
ISBN: 9781922175168 (paperback)
Subjects: Canberra (Paddle Steamer)--History.
           Paddle steamers--Australia.
           Paddle steamers--Australia--History..
           Other Authors/Contributors:
           Garfield, Peter, author.
Dewey Number: 623.8243

Printed in China
Cover design by David Khan
Typeset by Wanissa Somsuphangsri

BE PUBLISHED

Publish Through a Successful Publisher. National Distribution, Macmillan & International Distribution to the United Kingdom, North America. Sales Representation to South East Asia
Email: markzocchi@brolgapublishing.com.au

Paddle Steamers of Australia

P.S. Canberra - The First Hundred Years

Beth Conner

with Captain Peter Garfield

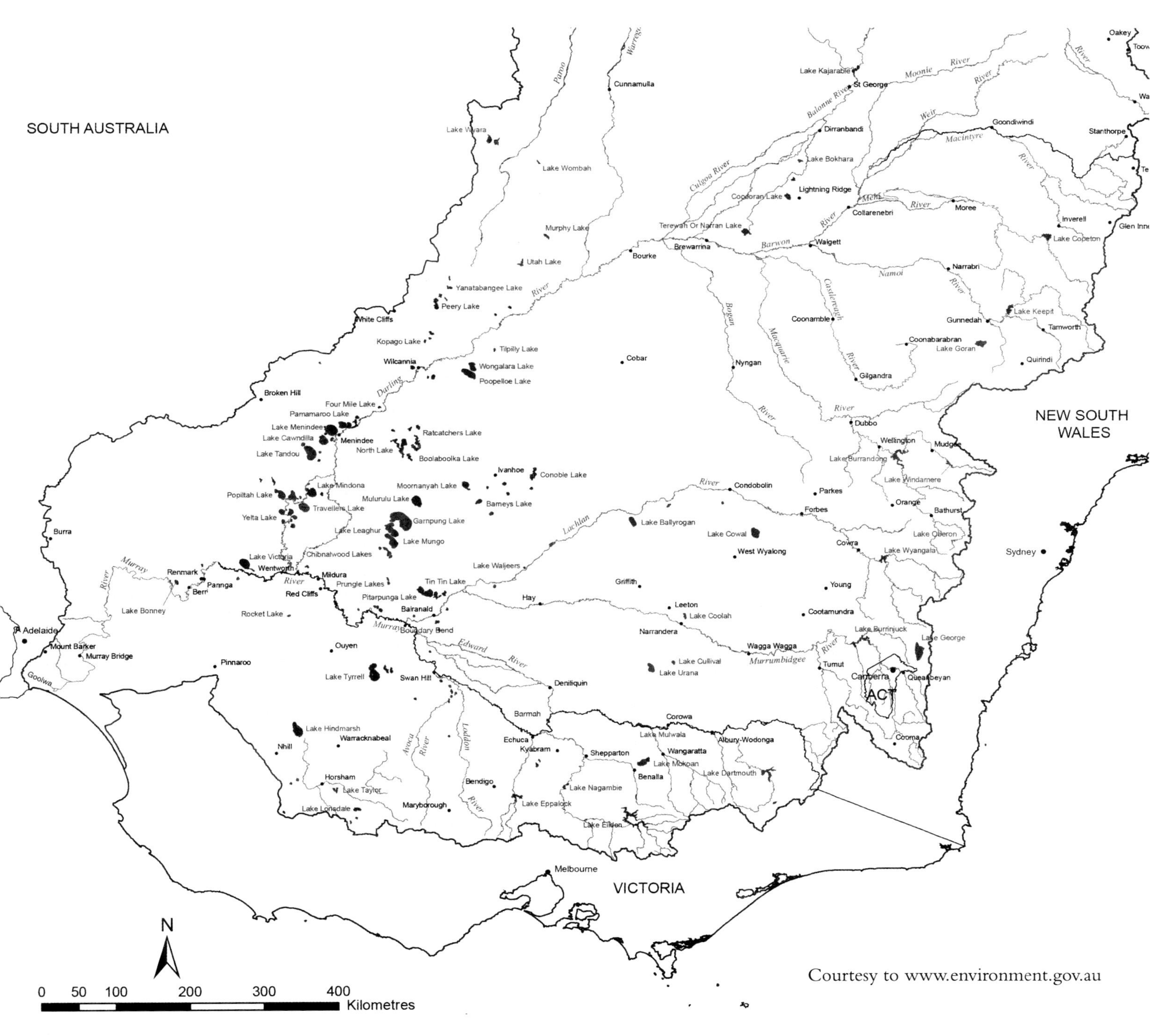

SOUTH AUSTRALIA
NEW SOUTH WALES
VICTORIA
ACT
Adelaide
Mount Barker
Murray Bridge
Goolwa
Pinnaroo
Burra
Renmark
Pannga
Berri
Lake Bonney
Rocket Lake
Ouyen
Nhill
Warracknabeal
Horsham
Lake Taylor
Lake Lonsdale
Maryborough
Bendigo
Melbourne
Swan Hill
Lake Tyrrell
Lake Hindmarsh
Kyabram
Echuca
Barmah
Shepparton
Lake Nagambie
Lake Eppalock
Lake Eildon
Benalla
Lake Mokoan
Wangaratta
Albury-Wodonga
Lake Mulwala
Corowa
Lake Dartmouth
Deniliquin
Barham
Lake Cullival
Lake Urana
Narrandera
Wagga Wagga
Tumut
Cootamundra
Young
Leeton
Lake Coolah
Hay
Griffith
West Wyalong
Lake Cowal
Lake Ballyrogan
Condobolin
Forbes
Parkes
Orange
Bathurst
Cowra
Lake Oberon
Lake Wyangala
Sydney
Canberra
Queanbeyan
Cooma
Lake George
Lake Burrinjuck
Lake Windamere
Lake Burrandong
Wellington
Mudgee
Dubbo
Gilgandra
Coonabarabran
Lake Goran
Quirindi
Tamworth
Gunnedah
Lake Keepit
Narrabri
Coonamble
Nyngan
Cobar
Lake Copeton
Inverell
Glen Inne
Te
Wa
Stanthorpe
Goondiwindi
Moree
Collarenebri
Walgett
Brewarrina
Bourke
Lightning Ridge
Coodoran Lake
Terewah Or Narran Lake
Dirranbandi
Lake Bokhara
St George
Lake Kajarabie
Cunnamulla
Oakey
Toow
Boolaboolka Lake
North Lake
Menindee
Lake Menindee
Lake Cawndilla
Lake Tandou
Pamamaroo Lake
Four Mile Lake
Broken Hill
White Cliffs
Kopago Lake
Wilcannia
Tilpilly Lake
Wongalara Lake
Poopelloe Lake
Ratcatchers Lake
Ivanhoe
Conoble Lake
Moornanyah Lake
Barneys Lake
Garnpung Lake
Lake Mungo
Lake Leaghur
Mulurulu Lake
Lake Mindona
Popiltah Lake
Travellers Lake
Yelta Lake
Lake Victoria
Chibnalwood Lakes
Wentworth
Mildura
Red Cliffs
Prungle Lakes
Pitarpunga Lake
Tin Tin Lake
Balranald
Boundary Bend
Peery Lake
Yanatabangee Lake
Utah Lake
Murphy Lake
Lake Wombah
Lake Wivara
Lake Waljeers
Murray
River
Murray
River
Darling
River
Lachlan
River
Edward
River
Murrumbidgee
River
Avoca
River
Loddon
River
Campaspe
River
Bogan
Macquarie
River
Castlereagh
River
Namoi
River
Barwon
Macintyre
Weir
River
Moonie
River
Culgou River
Mehi
River
Warrego
Parroo
Kilometres
0 50 100 200 300 400
N
Courtesy to www.environment.gov.au

Courtesy of Conner Family Archives. Edited by Bruce Clark.

There is an old saying: Never let the truth get in the way of a good yarn. Many accounts of Australian history tell 'a good yarn'. The stories evolve around an object and value is placed on the importance and integrity of that particular thing. This is the story of an object, the *P.S. Canberra,* the families who kept her, the people who worked on her and the places she influenced.

The Boundary Bend Years

The story of why the *P.S. Canberra* was built begins with a family and a throwaway line. Someone in a small shop said: "There's money to be made on the river." The Conner family took this to heart and began traversing the Murray-Darling Basin in the late 1800s. For the most part they operated in and out of the Murrumbidgee and Murray rivers around the small town of Boundary Bend in Northern Victoria. The Conner brothers, John David (David) and Archibald Henry (Arch) were just two of the many fishermen along the rivers during the early 1900s.

The story of the brothers mother, Sarah and her husband William is one that is not uncommon to the times. William was a fisherman living in Swan Reach and had taught his sons to do the same. Between Sarah and William, they had ten children, seven surviving to adulthood. It was with William that David and Arch built their first paddle steamer, the *Nelson*. Even in those early days, the family worked together to make a living from fishing. So far as can be found, there is only one photo of William Conner. It shows that fishing and the river was a large part of life for the entire family.

As David and Arch grew up, they ventured out and purchased their own vessels and started fishing the wa-

(From Left) Sarah, Lucy, David and Arch Conner on the *Fairy* 1911. Taken in Boundary Bend.
Courtesy of the Conner Family Collection.

William is on the left of the row boat.

ters further upstream from Swan Reach. Between them, they purchased a vessel by the name of *Fairy*. While the brothers were off making their fortune, William had become somewhat dependent on alcohol. In 1911, after borrowing money from David for a journey to Adelaide, Sarah returned to Swan Reach only to be told by her husband: "You can get out and you can take Lucia (Lucy, their youngest daughter) with you." Having nowhere else to go, Sarah called on her sons. David and Arch returned to Swan Reach to retrieve their mother and sister.

Eileen, Lucy's daughter, said her mother was only about eight years old at the time. David was the main instigator in collecting the women, but Arch always kept an eye on them as well. At some point during that time, the Salvation Army became a large part of the Conner family, with Arch and his little brother William Jnr converting to the Salvation Army faith. Soon after, Sarah also converted as her sons had. This resulted in the red and white paint scheme (the Salvation Army colours) for the eventual vessel, the *P.S. Canberra*.

David, Arch, Sarah and Lucy worked and lived on the small vessels they owned at the time, making life cramped and uncomfortable. They would make dough on board and then, whenever they moored, they would use hollowed out trees as chimneys to cook it. Eileen said that considering the limited resources they had, they ate well enough. In stories passed through the Conner family, it is clear that they were resourceful

This grave card for William Jnr shows how much the family cared for their siblings. Before his death, he had worked on the boats with David and Arch.

when it came to food. They dined on various meats caught along the way, such as rabbits, wild pigs, ducks and the sort. The family relied on what they could catch and see, rather than what the few shops they saw offered. They were survivors. Whenever they weren't working on board, the brothers would go ashore and cut their own wood, rather than purchasing from the wood stacks along the river. Arch always said that: "…the people who owned the woodpiles on the river charged too much for us." Sarah and Lucy would attend to the 'household' duties, such as cooking and sewing and keeping the boat tidy.

The *PS Fairy*, with Sarah (right) and Lucy (left) standing on the front.

The family had started to amass some wealth and more of the Conner siblings joined the four on board. To compensate for the growth of family members on the boat, David and Arch purchased other vessels to add to their expanding fishing fleet. By this time, Arch had purchased his own paddle steamer the *P.S. Etona* and had started fishing for himself. Although being partially separated by water, the pair still combined their efforts whenever they needed to, with family being of great importance to them.

SS Canberra under construction in Goolwa, South Australia. In the background of the picture is another vessel belonging to the Conner brothers, the *P.S. Viola*. Courtesy of Conner Family Archives.

Midway through 1912, David decided that he would commission the building of a paddle steamer unique to his circumstances. With the inflow of money from the other vessels, David enlisted David Milne and his son to create a vessel for him. Milne had also constructed the *P.S. Etona* that Arch owned. The vessel would be unique for the time. Not only was it built during the decline of the paddle steamer era, but was designed to accommodate a family. Sarah and Lucy left the vessel and went to Nyah to live with another family member, George Alexander (Alic). David took one of the vessels, the *Viola*, to Goolwa in South Australia to begin building what would become the *P.S. Canberra*, though the family called her the *SS Canberra*.

August 2, 1913, the *SS Canberra*, was launched in Goolwa, South Australia. Her Marshall steam engine and cabins were installed once she was afloat. From there, the *Canberra*, with David at the helm, made her journey upstream to the waters in southern New South Wales. During the time between her launch in 1913 and when she was sold to the Collins family in 1944, the *Canberra* travelled distances as far as Hay on the Murrumbidgee in NSW, to Pooncarie on the Darling in NSW, and to Swan Reach on the Murray in South Australia with great regularity.

It is incalculable how many kilometres the *Canberra* travelled in her early life.

On the return to Nyah, David retrieved his mother and sister. With Lucy and Sarah now living on the *Canberra* with David and Arch working on the *Etona*, the family worked as a unit and became a highly successful fishing family. Between the members of the family, they held several properties between Nyah and Mildura as well as having nine paddle steamers over the years they were active. This became the heritage of the Conner family. In a journal kept by David he remarks: "May 9th, 1921: Just 30 years since we came on the Murray." Although the river was in their blood as was the love of the riverboats the river wasn't always a forgiving livelihood. There were closed seasons for fishing as well as summer often drying out the river completely. The properties along the river subsidised the off seasons for the paddle steamers and ensured the continuation of the family's wealth and prominence.

1914 saw a great change for the family as well as the world. A drought saw many boats that were still operating to be left high and dry. This caused an obvious drop in business for the family and they invested in lands in and around Boundary Bend becoming orchardists, growing mainly oranges and grapes. This in itself was no easy feat as water was scarce. Using steam engines as pumps, the Conner family were able to move what little water there was onto the lands that they owned. It was a challenging time for the inland communities of

Country Intelligence.

From our own Correspondents.

GOOLWA, AUGUST 4th.

The new steamer built by Messrs. Milne and Son was successfully launched on Saturday afternoon. She was named after our federal capital, Canberra. This boat has been built to the order of the Connor Bros. for fishing in the Murray. The cabins and machinery will be installed at an early date. Two more motor boats will be added to the already large fleet. Mr. Fletcher is having his sailing yacht fitted with an engine. and Mr. H. Godfrey has just built a fine boat to be fitted with a 5-h. p. engine.

Courtesy of the Trove
www.trove.nla.gov.au

Australia as all of the rivers were mostly dry with only small pockets of water remaining.

Aside from the fiscal challenges for the family, there was a great risk for the boats themselves, as being dry for too long made it more likely for the vessel to sink when the water finally did return. The *Canberra* was lucky in that she was not neglected. The family worked hard to mud-up her hull, to prevent the hull from drying and cracking. They did the same for the other vessels they owned at the time, including the *Etona* and the *Ranger.* The Conner family kept a close eye on their boats as they were a major part of their income. Unfortunately, after the 1914-1915 drought, most commercial vessels ended their time on the water because of neglect during that period. 1915 saw the River Murray Waters Agreement signed by the governments of Australia. This was about the management and sharing of waters of the River Murray and provided funds for the construction of a number of water storages, weirs and locks. It ensured that some water would remain in the river throughout the year, rather than being completely dry as had happened in 1914. The year also saw the Returned Soldiers' Settlement Act be passed and this would later impact much of the areas around Boundary Bend as well as influence the Conner family. Lands along the Murray River were divided up and given to soldiers to farm so that they had an income when they returned from service.

The front of a postcard written by David Conner.

This is a snap of our boat. high and dry on a sand spit near Mildura in 1914 drought. when the river stopped running for six months   It was middle of June that year before we floated off. (Dingy is on dry sand) Sand is banked round hull to prevent timber shrinking to much

Postcard written by David Conner to an unknown person explaining about the *PS Canberra*'s situation during 1914.

John David Conner.

John David Conner

Born March 24, 1878.
Died October 1, 1941.

John David Conner was known to his family and friends simply as David. He was the original owner of the *P.S. Canberra* and according to his journal and interviews with his brother Arch, he was a proper man for the most part, although he did write about journeys 'to the races' on various occasions.

Family was very important to David and he was constantly keeping notes on where the family was and what they were up to. During the time David was alive he lived with his mother on board and for a time, his sister Lucy. He also had many friends along the river. The Scadding family, the O'Bree family and a man by the name of Mick Bath, who presumably worked on the vessel with both David and Arch. From the pages of his journal, David is obviously a hard worker. He made notes of nets that were being made, when the nets were being tarred and what fish were pulled out of the water.

On his death, David's obituary stated he was: "A well-known and respected resident of Boundary Bend where he had lived for the past 30 years following the occupation of a fisherman on the Murray River and was the owner of the fishing steamer *Canberra*."

John David Conner aboard the *P.S. Canberra* circa 1916.
Taken in Boundary Bend present day location of the 1228 kilometre marker.
Courtesy of the Conner Family Archive.

The *P.S. Canberra* being kept alongside the *P.S. Etona* at Boundary Bend. Circa 1916.

When water finally returned to the Murray, the Conner family boats were re-floated with great care so as not to damage the hulls and they returned to fishing the water when fish stocks were back to normal. Once again, the family prospered. In an interview with Arch, he says that other fishermen referred to them as: 'Top notch fishermen' and 'Pelicans', and that he and his brother: "…really knew how to catch them." However, their vessels weren't used just as fishing boats. The *Canberra* in particular was used for many different tasks, including carrying light cargo and livestock. The greatest industry for the boats though was the haulage of fish using large hoop nets, or drum nets. The nets were constructed from string and tarred to help prevent rotting while sitting in the water.

P.S. Canberra hauling sheep.
Courtesy of Conner Family Archives.

1920s *Canberra* and fishing nets, Boundary Bend.
Courtesy of Conner Family Archives.

1922 *P.S. Canberra* steamed up. Unknown location.
Courtesy of Conner Family Archives.

When spring rains eventually returned the Murray River to a navigable height, David would take the *Canberra* to Swan Hill where he would pick up grocery orders from Permewan Wright, a wholesaler of various produce and products. These orders were for stores along the Murrumbidgee River and into Balranald and Hay. The *Canberra,* being light and small was able to navigate waters far sooner than the larger vessels that went up to Hay, such as the *Pevensey* and the *Success.* During these journeys, David would note in his diary which boats were where and whether they were loaded or not.

"August 29, 1921: *Pevensey* went up with *Echuca* barge. *Ulonga* came down with *Ada* barge."

P.S. Success towing a barge on the Murrumbidgee River, circa 1911.
The Conner men stand on the side of the *Maud*, the *Ranger*'s chimney just in view.
Courtesy of the State Library of South Australia, Godson Collection.

Fishing on the Murray-Darling Basin

The Murray-Darling was once the major highway for bringing food productions and wool to the major cities of the country. Hundreds of vessels worked in and out of the ports along the rivers and tributaries. Many of these boats were small fishing vessels known as a mosquito fleet. The vessels were small, easy to manoeuvre and could go further upstream and downstream than the larger more well-known vessels. The Conner brothers had one such fleet with which to run their fishing business. There were several methods of fishing in the day, the most efficient of which, was drum nets. These drum nets were specifically constructed and made for fishing. The main barrel of the net would have hoops of steel for the drum with wings made of string. One end of the wings would be stitched to the hoop, the other end tied to a sapling. The saplings would measure to be about ten foot long, often one of them was longer than the other, though not always necessary. Each net had to have the registration number on the peg above water. The size of the mesh for the nets had to be legal size or the fisheries would confiscate the nets. The nets would then be tarred in large pots to help prevent rotting whilst in the water. Making a new net would take roughly a week. David Conner had a licence for around 100 drum nets.

After the fish were caught, they were kept alive in specifically designed, enclosed sunken punts for transport to the markets. The mosquito fleets would often utilise the larger boats whose journeys to major ports were more regular and tie the punts across the sponson decks to be sent to market. David and his brother Arch were something of a tandem team, one boat heading to market, while the other continued to check the nets. Unlike some of the other fisherman around the Murray River, the Conner

(From left) *P.S. Maud*, *P.S. Austria* and *P.S. Fairy*. Note the front of the *Fairy* is covered in saplings. These are the poles used to hold fishing drum nets in place. Courtesy of the State Library of South Australia, Godson Collection.

brothers would check the nets every eight hours or so. The measurements of fish were counted in baskets and pounds. At certain stages through the years, fish prices reached £9 per pound weight. The prices for fish helped the Conner brothers amass a large fortune.

In David's journal, he writes about the various occasions that he would tar nets, how many baskets he and his brother would take from the river as well as keeping his eye on prices of fish. Most interestingly, David made notes of weather, river heights and what paddle steamers were where. His journal provides details of what life was like at that time.

There are few of the mosquito fleet fishing vessels left today alhough, three exist in Echuca that once belonged to the Conner brothers. The *P.S. Canberra*, the *P.S. Etona* and the *P.S. Ranger*. All three are privately owned, though the *P.S. Canberra* is still commercially run as a tourist vessel.

The sunken boat on the side of the *Canberra* are the punts to keep the fish alive.
On the roof are some of the loops of metal for a drum net.
Courtesy of the Conner Family Archives.

As with millions of families throughout the world, the Conner family was deeply impacted by the war. Arch and his younger brother Alic joined the army and they were shipped out to France in 1917. Arch joined up as a result of the death of his first wife in childbirth. Both mother and child were buried in Balranald and Arch was left on the *Etona* on his own. Becoming depressed from the tragic loss, he decided to join his brother Alic in enlisting in the army. The two were stationed together, though given separate jobs. Alic was a rifleman and Arch, a stretcher bearer. The two kept the family spirit alive, spending much of their time together, including being reprimanded for disobeying orders.

Wedding photo of Alic and Mary Bell Stewart.
Courtesy of the Conner Family Archieves

OFFENCE- Conduct to the prejudice of good order and Military discipline in that he neglected to put on his web equipment after being ordered to do so. Durrington 17.8.17
AWARD- 4 days F.P.No. 2 with forfeiture of 28 days pay. By Capt. T.B. STEELE 17.8.17
TOTAL FORFEITURE- 28 days pay
Pay Book No. 269818/16

CONNER	George Alexander (Pte)	3044.	7/39th.Btn.
Surname.	Other Names.	Regimental No.	Unit.
PURPORT.			AUTHORITY.
Emb. at Melb.per "Ballarat" on 19/2/17.			
26/4/17 Mshd into 10th Trng.Bn. Durrington from Australia			LDN.33/2-17
Pay Book No. 269818/16			RTO 39/9-17
1/9/17 T.O.S of 39th Btn from 7th Rfcts 39th Btn ex 3rd A.D.B.D			RTO 29/2-17
20/8/17 Proceeded Overseas to France ex No 12 Camp Durrington via Southampton			LON 45/1-17
BURIED MERICOURT L ABR's COM CEM EXTENSION 3¾ MILES E. N.E of CORBIE		(V.T)	LON 57/18
26/4/18 KILLED IN ACTION	(VT)		RTO 19/1-18

Excerpts from Alic's war records.
Courtesy of the Australian Defence Force Archives (ADFA).
Retrieved by Sue Conner.

World War One brought tragedy to many families including the Conner family. Alic was killed in action on April 26, 1918 at Mericourt L'abbe, where he was later interred.

Talking to Arch's grandchildren, they said that he rarely if ever spoke about his time in the army. Arch was mentioned in dispatches in late 1919, though for what is somewhat of an unofficial version. The story in the family is that Arch, having been a stretcher bearer for his battalion, went to the line and retrieved his brother Alic, returning him to barracks, where Alic later died. Letters exchanged between the War Offices and Sarah whilst she was aboard the *Canberra,* show the story of how the words on Alic's grave were decided upon. She also explains the death of Alic's remarried wife and the death of William, later in 1918. The letters also give an insight into how life was for her aboard the boat. David wrote to the War Offices requesting photos of his brother's grave. Even separated by such a distance, the family kept each other in mind. Letters and postcards were common for the family as it was how they kept in touch. These are just some of the many that are held by the family and in archives.

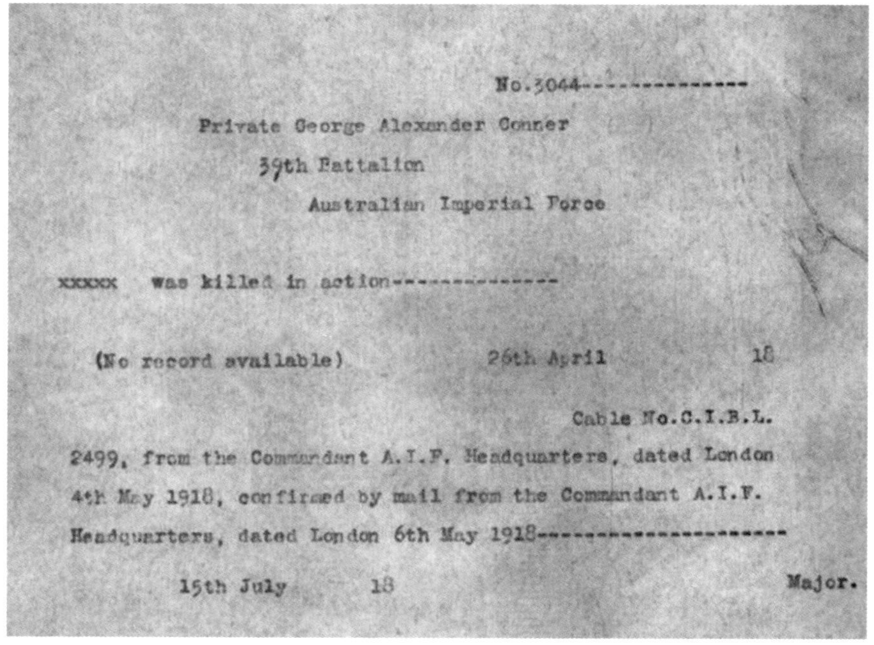

SWAN REACH, December 3.—Mr. W. Conner, an old and respected resident of Swan Reach, died recently at the age of 82. He had been suffering from asthma for two years, but was not confined to this bed. He had lived at Swan Reach for 23 years, and had been a fisherman for 30 years. Previous to his coming to the Murray he kept a store in Lilydale, Victoria, and he also ran a sawmill at Wandon. He left a widow, three daughters, and two sons, 13 grandchildren, and one great-grandchild.

Monday December 8, 1918, The Advertiser.
Retrieved from Trove.

No.3044

Private George Alexander Conner

39th Battalion

Australian Imperial Force

xxxxx   was killed in action

(No record available)   26th April   18

                                    Cable No.C.I.B.L.
2499, from the Commandant A.I.F. Headquarters, dated London
4th May 1918, confirmed by mail from the Commandant A.I.F.
Headquarters, dated London 6th May 1918

        15th July   18   Major.

The note received by Sarah on the death of her son Alic.

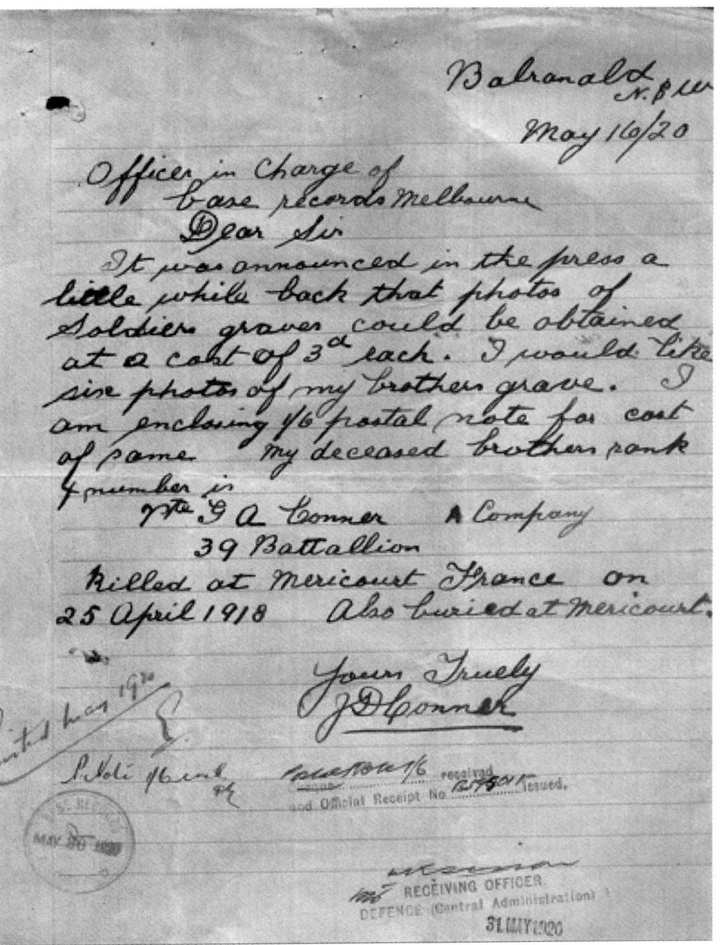

Letter to the War Offices from David Conner.
Courtesy of Australian Defence Force Archives.

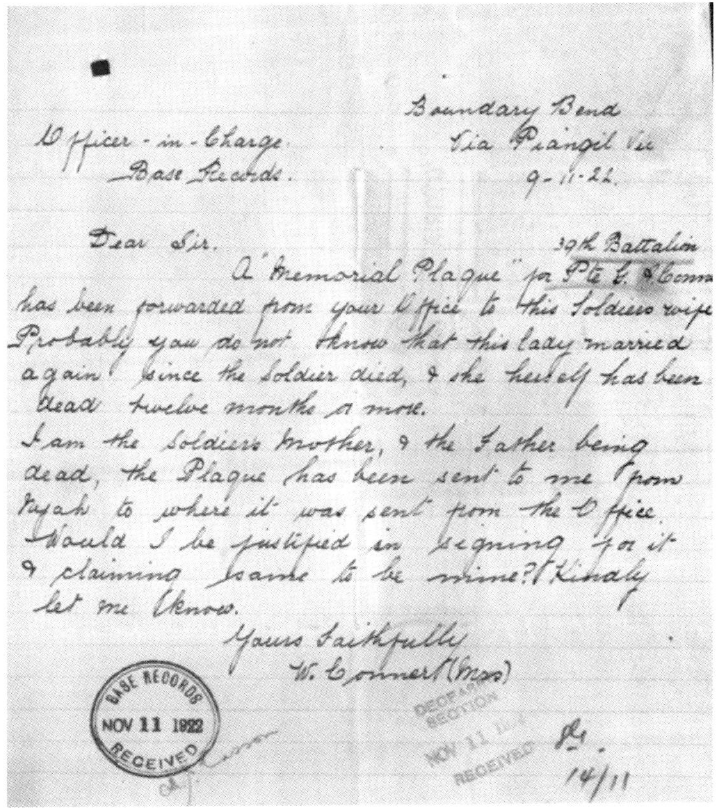

Letter written from Sarah.
Courtesy of the ADFA.

Babranald
may 1- 19 23

dear Sir
i am sorrey i could not
send the form in be fore
as i live far out in the
countery we have to wate
a good wile for mails and
be fore we can send them
a way. i did not git the other
form you sent to me i shall
be sorrey if i am to late to
have it don

yours truely
Sd. Conner
S.S. Canberra
Babranald   N.S. Wailes

Letter to the War Offices from Sarah Conner.
Courtesy of the Australian Defence Force Archives.

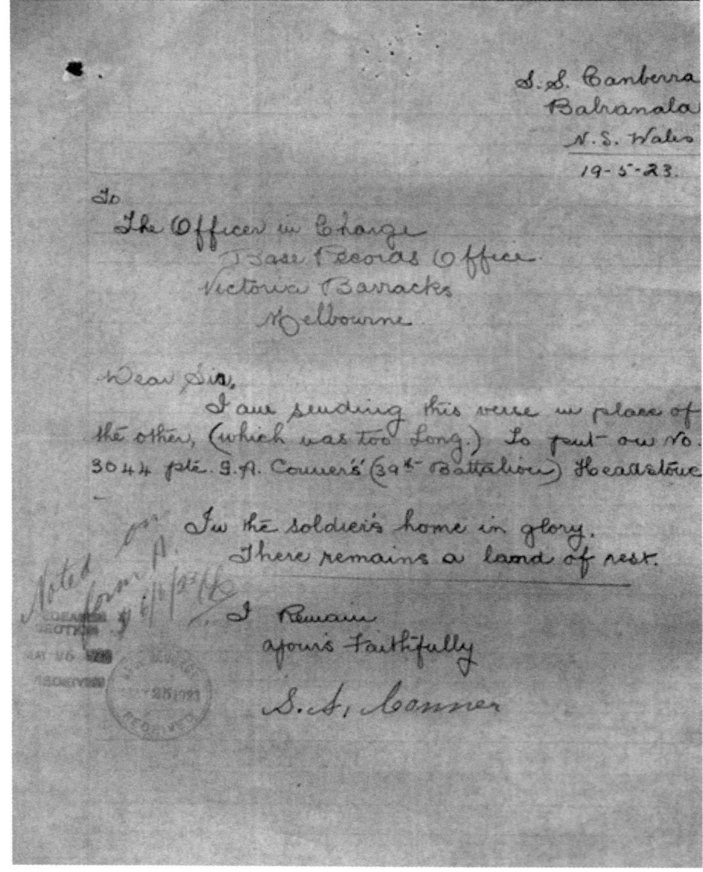

S.S. Canberra
Babranald
N.S. Wales
19-5-23.

To
The Officer in Charge
Base Records Office
Victoria Barracks
Melbourne

Dear Sir,
I am sending this verse in place of
the other, (which was too long.) to put on No.
3044 Pte. G.A. Conner's (39th Battalion) Headstone

In the soldier's home in glory.
There remains a land of rest.

I Remain
yours faithfully
S.A. Conner

Letter to the War Offices from Sarah Conner.
Courtesy of the Australian Defence Force Archives.

Comparison of the grave markers for Alic.
Courtesy of Peter Garfield (Left) and Frank Conner (Right)

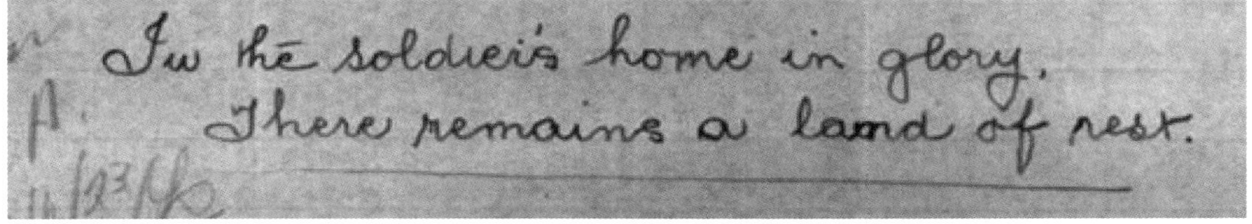

Above, Sarah's words that are now inscribed on George's grave in France.

Whilst his brothers were at war, David continued his work on the river with his mother and sister helping him. He spent much of his time up and down the Murrumbidgee and Murray Rivers fishing the waters. He also developed a new type of net for the fishing industry that helped cut down fish death during transportation. Although David and his family were relatively prosperous, owning properties from Nyah to Mildura, the family was no stranger to tragedy. During her lifetime Sarah had ten children but only seven lived to adulthood. Of the seven, one died in World War One, another died of cholera. In the time she was alive, Sarah lived on nine different paddle steamers, rarely having earth beneath her.

It wasn't until 1919 that things started to return to normal for the Conner family. Arch had returned to a Soldier Settlement that he took up in Boundary Bend. It became a regular place for paddle steamers to come in and out of. David and Arch were again working together continuing the balance of fishing and growing crops on the land. Not only this, they worked together on shifting cargo that was hard for the larger vessels to hold in conjunction with their regular loads. On one such occasion in 1929, the *Canberra* was used to shift a large drilling rig for a lock construction up river. The *Canberra*, the *Etona* and another vessel they owned, the *Ranger* became their major vessels with which to fish. They made plenty of money and caught a huge amount of fish, despite the misgivings of some in the waters around Balranald. However, the homeport of the Conner brothers was Boundary Bend where they had finally settled. Arch remarried and had five children with Louisa Anne Dobson. David remained a bachelor all his life and had no children. Even after all those years on the river, the family remained relatively close. David always made special mention in his journal of what his family was doing. One particular entry sums up the connection of the family: "December 25, 1921: Christmas Day. All together in Boundary Bend."

The place that David, Arch and the rest of the Conner family called home in Boundary Bend is still in the hands of the descendants of those original fishermen. Walking onto the property, there are remnants of the past, with photos of the old days hanging on the walls as a reminder and homage to their lives.

The end of the Boundary Bend chapter of the *Canberra's* life, came with David's death on September 1, 1941 aged 63. He was buried in the Swan Hill cemetery alongside his mother, Sarah, who had died the previous year. Despite holding on to the boat for as long as he could, Arch sold the *Canberra* to the Collins family and A. E. Silbereisen in 1944.

This was the fate of many vessels along the Murray-Darling Basin. The above photo is of a vessel from the mosquito fishing fleet. The name of the boat is still under debate.
Courtesy of Trove.

The Mildura Years

When the *Canberra* arrived in Mildura, the homeport for the Collins brothers, she was in a derelict state. It was during the 1940s and 50s that she was rebuilt and returned to her former glory. The *Canberra* was one of several in the family fleet, others included the *Kookaburra,* the *Excelsior* and the *Alpha*. The Collins Brothers were skilled in the work they did and taught many other shipwrights the craft. They were born and raised on the river along with their two sisters.

Norm Collins making repairs to the boiler on the *P.S. Canberra*. This was taken in Mildura during the 1950s.
On the right hand side of the boat there are tools and planks of wood to be used in repairs.
The engine seen here is the original engine used by the Conner brothers, as is the steering wheel.

Bill Collins

Born November 9, 1907.
Died October 17, 1989.

The Collins brothers and indeed their family were synonymous with the Murray River. They took hold of many different paddle steamers and restored them. Although they used the *P.S. Canberra* for a relatively short time (1944 to 1966) compared to some of their other boats, their ambitions for the vessel ensured the continued usage of the *Canberra* for the first one hundred years of her life. Although she didn't meet the brothers' ambitions of a tourist vessel in Mildura she did pioneer the idea of short pleasure cruises for tourists along the Murray River.

In a memoir by their sister Pearl Wallace (nee Collins), she recounts many stories of her brothers and how they worked together. One such story is of the brothers handing each other snakes as a practical joke. The pair worked together for the majority of their lives, leaving behind a well-used heritage of riverboats in Mildura. Pearl Wallace writes about how her brothers would give people "merciless hell" when they were aboard the boats. It was a trait that both Norm and Bill would be remembered for. Pearl also remembered that Bill was a champion life-saver, having rescued fifteen people from drowning.

Bill Collins at the wheel of the *P.S. Canberra*
Courtesy of the State Library of South Australia.
Godson Collection.

Norm Collins

Born 21st of November, 1908.
Died 10th of August, 1982.

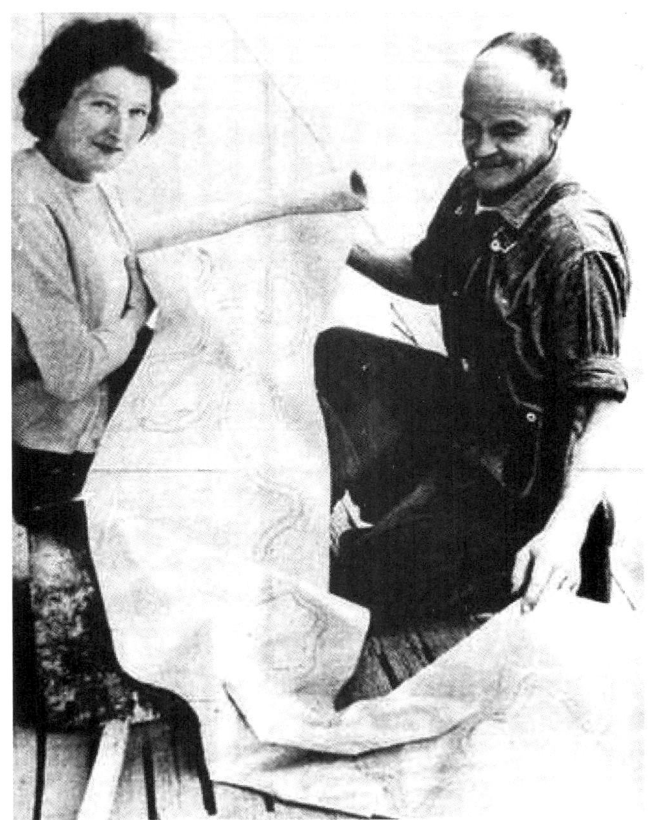

Norm Collins and his wife Hazel.
Courtesy of the State Library of South Australia.
Godson Collection.

With financial aid from A. E. Silbereisen, Norm and Bill Collins managed to make the *P.S. Canberra* water worthy and able to carry passengers in late 1944. The full extent of Silbereisen's involvement is difficult to track. What is known is that his aim was to have the *Canberra* able to carry passengers over the 1944 Christmas period. The boat was given a provisional permit to carry 50 passengers on the main deck by the Director of Navigation J.K. Davis. With records from the *Sunraysia Daily,* the *Canberra* is known to have run on Boxing Day of 1944. She continued to run through the school holidays of 1944 and 1945.

The Collins brothers ran the *Canberra* with various people captaining her and managing the vessel.

They were always remembered by the various skippers, engineers and other river families as being very open and caring. They spent a considerable amount of money on advertising pleasure cruises alongside their vessel the *Showboat Avoca.* It was the beginning of the *Canberra's* life as a tourist vessel. She was used for camping and fishing trips and these trips were a great success as most people were looking for a good time during the war years.

Sometime during this period a second deck was added to the top of the *Canberra.* The exact date for this alteration is unknown, with only a rough time period of the late 40s as a suggestion. According to local historian Helen Coulson, it was during 1949

Boxing Day Holiday

Many district residents spent the Boxing Day holiday swimming, fishing, boating or picnicking by the river. The p.s. Avoca took two loads of picnickers to a shady rendezvous at Whirlpool Bend (opposite the 810 mile tree, the distance being measured from Albury). It was at this point said Captain Treacy, that the "Premier Barge" took a nose dive on a flooded river and sank in the spring of 1923. The p.s. Canberra also took a large crowd downtream through the lock to a picnic ground in the direction of Merbein. A very large crowd visited the Merbein races. Because of counter attractions yesterday, Mildura hotels and clubs did not experience any excessive demand. But, the booth at the Merbein race meeting disposed of its quota long before the last race was run, and patrons were buying soft drinks towards the close of the day.

...pect plenty of lively entertainment.

Trips By P.S. Canberra

The 150-ton paddle steamer Canberra, with a passenger accommodation of 100, will make a three-day trip up the river, leaving on Boxing Day. This will enable local residents to spend a few days at ideal fishing spots and camping sites. It is proposed to make trips on New Year's Day. Captain N. Collins, who will be in charge of the steamer, is well-known along the Murray River for his navigation ability. Persons wishing to charter the boat for any length of time should contact Mr L. Lee-Proops, at Burton's Motors.

Open Events.

THREE-DAY FISHING AND CAMPING TRIP
To Wentworth by P.S. Canberra
ON SATURDAY NEXT

Camping space available on boat if necessary.　　Return fare 15/.

Day Trip For Wentworth Residents
SUNDAY, DECEMBER 31.　　　SIX HOURS' CRUISE.

Three hours at picnic ground. Fare 6/.

Boiling water supplied.　　　Soft drinks obtainable on boat.

BOOKINGS — BURTON'S MOTORS.　　PHONE 599.

Excerpts taken from *Sunraysia Daily,* from December,1944, Courtesy of the State Library of Victoria.

that the promenade deck was added. She states that the top deck was: "almost certainly [added] during 1949." However, there is evidence to suggest that the date was earlier, as in an advertisement in December 19, 1944, the *Canberra* was listed to hold 100 passengers for a camping trip. The addition of the top deck allowed the boat to accommodate more passengers on cruises, a necessity with the beginnings of the tourism industry involving historic paddle steamers.

The closure of the RAAF base at Mildura at the war's end saw the *Canberra* almost idle again. Bill Collins took over the *Avoca*, *Canberra's* competitor, in 1949, and concentrated on running her. *Canberra's* owner, A. E. Silbereisen, finally completed the registration of the vessel in December 1949.

It wasn't until 1950 that the *Canberra* was officially registered and the first survey ticket was given. Bill Hogg, son of skipper Captain Hillary 'Paddy' Hogg, recalls carving the registration number behind the helm when his father ran the boat. By 1950 Ernie Randell was noted as Master of the vessel on the Survey Certificate. By this time the promenade deck was built and the main deck roof was extended back over the stern. Silbereisen was issued with another survey certificate on December 1, 1950 stating that the *Canberra* was allowed to carry 66 passengers and that the boiler could run at 80 pounds per square inch steam pressure.

By 1952 the *Canberra* was moored at Renmark in South Australia. Paddy Hogg and his young family took

Paddy Hogg at the helm of the *Canberra*

over and began working her once more. Paddy secured a contract to supply timber piles for the sheet piling upstream of the Renmark wharf for 25 pounds each. Paddy used the skills learnt during his days on the logging boats at Echuca. The timber piles were felled and dressed on the riverbank. Ropes were then tied to the piles and they were dragged down the bank using the paddle shaft as a winch. Outrigger logs were placed across the bow through the windows of the sunken cabin 'dining room'. Two piles could be chained to each side of the outriggers. On a 1953 survey certificate Captain Hogg is shown as the managing owner.

During the fruit picking season Paddy ran a Sunday lunch cruise for the mainly Italian pickers: fifteen bob for a four hour cruise. They would cruise up the river to a fisherman's hut where Paddy would have a sheep on a spit cooking. Paddy supplied the liquid refreshments, probably sourced from Angoves winery where he worked when the timber contract finished.

Pendle's Coaches organised a cruise on the *Canberra* during Paddy's time working for Angoves. Paddy couldn't leave work so he organised George Aldridge, a local steam man, to run the boiler leaving Paddy's son Bill free to drive the boat. George wasn't convinced an

P.S. Canberra moored in Renmark during the early 1950's

11 year old was ready for command but Paddy told him, "You just keep feeding the logs in!" The cruise went off without a hitch until word of the young captain's achievement made it back to the local postmaster Bill Drage. Bill was a former riverboat captain of some repute who was a stickler for the rules. Bill informed the authorities at the Marine and Harbours Board who were quickly asking for explanations. Paddy managed to assure the surveyor that he was asleep down the front cabin during the cruise and the case was dropped.

P.S. Canberra in Mildura during the 1960s, likely just before leaving for Echuca

Paddy Hogg worked alongside Bill and Norm Collins and tells a story about his time with the brothers. In one particular instance, a boat named *Enterprise* was sold to another company. The boat had then become stuck and sunk at Cadell Rocks. The story continues that Norm was more than willing to help repair the boat. The *Enterprise* was returned to Mildura where Norm and Bill worked together to make the repairs more permanent. After being repaired, Norm and Bill took the *Enterprise* downstream to Mannum.

The *P.S. Canberra* coming in to Lock 11 on her regular cruises in and around Mildura

In 1953 Sir Robert George, Governor of South Australia, visited Renmark and went for a cruise along the river. Half of the population of Renmark seemed to be on the boat as it departed. There were 140 on board plus the Governor. This number was considerably higher than the 66 passengers noted on the survey certificate. *Canberra* was low in the water with all that weight and the normally dry planks above the waterline were leaking badly. Paddy skippered the boat while young Bill Hogg fired the boiler. Bill spent most of the trip underneath the deck working the bilge pumps.

In 1954 the Hogg's steamed the *Canberra* back to Mildura and Paddy found work at the Mildura Co-Op running the boilers. The Survey Certificate soon expired and as things were very quiet along the river, there seemed no need to renew it. The boat was moored at Apex Park at this time. Paddy was at work and Bill and his sisters were on board when one day a huge dust storm blew out of the desert. Almost immediately the stern mooring line snapped followed shortly afterwards by the head line. All sense of direction was lost as the dust screamed around and visibility dropped. Finally the anchor was deployed and the storm gradually moved on, leaving the boat stranded in the middle of the river. Bill was exhausted from all this drama and wasn't sure what to do till his sister pointed out that there was still water in the boiler and asked, "Couldn't we fire her up and steam her back?"

Paddy was still trying to pay off what he owed on the boat so to make an extra quid he started running Heads and Tails dice games. On Friday and Saturday nights the locals would come down to the *Canberra* to gamble on the green table on the promenade deck. The amount of money being wagered was staggering. Bill saw the local butcher and his mates take home over seven thousand pounds in winnings. A raid by the police bought things to a sudden halt.

Not long afterwards, when the boat was moored near *Slaughterhouse Reach* near Mildura, a Two Up game started up on the NSW side of the river. The punters would pay Bill to row them across to the game in the *Canberra's* dinghy. Paddy was in the centre of the action when once again the police raided. Men came flying out of the scrub pleading for Bill to row over and pick them up. When the burly coppers burst into view Bill decided discretion was the better part of valour. He hid in an empty drum until the din subsided. Paddy escaped without charge.

HE OWNS EXCELSIOR

I HAVE had a letter from Harold Roberts (23 17th street, Hillside), saying that the river steamer Excelsior now belongs to Bill Collins at Mildura. "Two years ago," he tells me, "Arthur White and I bought the steamer Ranger, and we had her alongside the Excelsior for four months. We refitted the Ranger, and have brought her down to Murray Bridge. Bill has told many thrilling stories about the "Ex." and the Alpha.

"The Collins family are renowned for their exploits on the River Darling. Bill's father used to fire the boiler, his mother steered, while Bill and his brother Norman, in their short-pants days, were given sole charge of the big barges.

"Many exciting times have they had, the two boys together, standing and pulling for all their young might on the giant steering wheels of the barge in breathless endeavor to round the hairpin bends of the narrow Darling at flood times."

Courtesy of Trove. From the Chronicle, Thursday 3rd May, 1945

Mildura in flood in 1956. The *P.S. Canberra* is in the right foreground.
Courtesy of Murray Darling Basin Authority

The 1956 floods saw many old river boats bought back into use but the *Canberra* remained moored at Mildura. Bill Collins sold the *Avoca* in 1957 and used his money to buy Paddy's share of the *Canberra*. The Hoggs moved on to the *Mayflower*. The Collin's re-roofed the promenade deck in aluminium for its light weight. One windy day the new roof peeled off like a sardine can lid. Losing her roof would happen to *Canberra* a number of times during the next few decades.

By the early 1960s tourism was beginning to grow. Better country roads led city people to head out along the beaten track. With their caravans in tow or in buses they headed along the river from Adelaide and over the ranges from Melbourne seeking a quiet spot to camp or some history to discover. The Pioneer Settlement at Swan Hill opened to huge crowds but the place to see the riverboats was Mildura. This created something of a 'heyday' for the *Canberra* and Mildura, as well as many areas along the Murray River. The Collins brothers began renovating the *Canberra* to meet the demand. In 1963 *Canberra* was slipped and her stem post replaced along with many planks in her bow. The sunken cabin was removed shortly after and the deck was re-laid using timber salvaged from the *Canally.*

Canberra operated successfully for the next few years at Mildura with the Collin's improving her each year. The only opposition was from Alby Pointon and the *Mayflower,* a much smaller boat that was diesel driven. The tables turned late in 1965 when Alby bought the former snagging steamer *Melbourne* to town from Echuca, making the *Canberra* almost redundant. With the top cabins removed and an open promenade deck added, *Melbourne* could carry far more people in comfort. Some of the locals around Mildura remember the Collins' would try to bribe the lockmaster with beer to prevent the *Melbourne* getting through. By this time, there were movements in Echuca seeking out a tourist attraction to make use of the historic wharf that was unused. In 1966 *Canberra* was slipped again and it was during this maintenance that a group of Echuca businessmen arrived in Mildura looking for a paddle steamer to buy.

When the Echuca Co-operative, consisting mostly of motel owners and various businessmen, arrived in Mildura, the Collins brothers were open to the idea of the *Canberra* being sent to Echuca to be used as a tourist boat. Bill's time with the *Canberra* was mostly over; however, Norm accompanied the vessel to Echuca on December 12, 1966. It was the last time the *Canberra* would see Mildura. As of the writing of this book, the *Canberra* has still not returned to Mildura.

The day before leaving for Echuca, the *Canberra* was struck by a storm. This caused the top deck to be swept onto the bank. What remained of the promenade deck was gathered and placed on top of the main roof. With the main deck unharmed, the vessel continued upstream to her, soon to be permanent homeport, Echuca. Knowing she would need to be repaired, Norm and his crew ordered for materials to be shipped to Koondrook where they could pick up the supplies and do repairs en route.

December 24, 1966. The *P.S. Canberra* arrives in Echuca, escorted by the *P.S. Etona*.
The two vessels reunited after being separated since being owned by the Conner brothers.

The night before leaving Mildura, there was large storm that demolished her top deck.

So far as can be found, the trip after the storm was relatively uneventful. The *P.S. Canberra* arrived in Echuca on December 24, 1966, escorted by the *P.S. Etona*, now owned by the Symonds family. The *P.S. Etona* and the *P.S. Canberra* were once again side by side as they had been fifty years previously.

(Left to right) Eddie Hazelman and Norm Collins in 1967

The Echuca Years

The *Canberra's* start in Echuca was a positive one. Within three days of her arrival, she had carried eight hundred passengers. The Echuca Syndicate looked after her under the watchful eye of Norm who had agreed to run the *Canberra* for them until other arrangements could be made. The *Canberra* was moored opposite the Hopwood Gardens where the *P.S. Adelaide* sat as a static display, the park was called Paddlewheel Park, although it is now known as River Boat Dock.

With people having the necessary skills to run the vessel in short supply, Norm stayed on longer than was agreed. Eventually, the time came for him to return to Mildura and the Echuca Syndicate were desperate for another qualified captain. Les Telley was hired in May 1967 and George Vickers, who would later captain the boat, was engineer. Ken Easdown and Des O'Reilly often filled in as deckhands. In these early days of the *Canberra's* time in Echuca, money was the biggest problem for her.

The Christmas Holidays of 1967 saw the boat carrying more passengers than the first year but the expenses were proving daunting. Running the vessel was a strain on the Syndicate and they worked hard to keep the business solvent. In 1968 a front page article in the *Riverine Herald* alleged the boat was about to be taken down river to Swan Hill where the Pioneer Settlement was doing a roaring trade. Many of the directors of the co-operative gave donations to keep the boat going. During these times when money was short Ken Easdown was often seen selling shares in the boat instead of attending to his day job of selling vacuum cleaners.

The community response to keep the little boat running was amazing. Local businessmen such as Roy Vincent, having been told their invoices could not be paid, wrote the debt off and donated more. Retired captains such as Buck Freeman and Don Tyler gave up their time to captain the vessel. The local Lions Club helped out as well. Reg Ford donated the use of his earthmoving equipment to haul the *Canberra* up the Moama slipway in 1969. This was the boat's first out of water inspection at Echuca and the report wasn't reassuring. The surveyor made it clear that quite a number of hull planks needed to be replaced. Money was tight, as always, and once again a number of directors reached for their cheque books to avert the crisis. Around this time the idea of leasing the boat was discussed, and quickly found favour with many directors, whose resources were becoming strained.

(From left) Laurie Sutton, Coralyn Yeaman, the two young girls are Coralyn's daughters, Melinda and Marisa, George Vickers, George 'Buck' Freeman and Eddie Hazleman. George Vickers was originally an engineer on the *Canberra* before sitting for his Masters' ticket and becoming skipper of the vessel.

It was during this time that George Vickers came aboard as an engineer. He later gained his skipper's ticket and became the main captain for the *Canberra* during the 1970s. He was to be the captain who returned the *Canberra* to a gambling house, though this time for a good cause. George and a local service club held gambling for charity charters that were very popular. These were black tie events that cost one hundred dollars to attend and raised $10,000 each time the event ran — a large amount of money for the times. Roulette, Black Jack and other games were the vices of the gambling nights that were held once a year. Only the captain and the president knew when the boat was going, so they could avoid police involvement. These occasions were highly successful and particularly well known for the amount of alcohol consumed and a good time had by all. However, the 1974 run would be the last. During this particular evening there was a couple sitting on the outside of the rails on the promenade deck. The pair fell overboard. The *Canberra* came about and they were quickly rescued. The sobering reality of what would have happened if they had drowned led to the event being held on land after that.

George Vickers:

George grew up on his Family's farm at Panoo, but grew to dislike the harsh farming life. The river and the river boat life were dear loves to George and he began working on the *P.S. Adelaide*. He was particularly fond of the *Adelaide*, always telling stories of how hard the engine worked. Seen as a 'true steam man' George was someone who had many stories about other river captains and fantastical stories of working on the river. One such story included a bullock team that had stopped because a goanna refused to move out the way. The man who was working the bullock team, tied the bullocks to the goanna to move it. From there, the bullocks were mysteriously whisked away up the tree, held fast by the chain that was attached to the goanna! Another story was that a fight broke out between a Murray Cod and a bullock team. They fought so hard that they managed to straighten out a bend of the river! These are just some of the yarns that George would tell about drunks, harsh skippers and trained birds that were spies for their masters. George was quoted as saying: "I never take life seriously. If there's a bit of fun about, I'll be in it."

Much of what George had learned came from Barney Binks, Captain of the *Adelaide* during George's time as engineer. Having listened carefully, George headed down to Melbourne and sat his captain's test. When George attained his skipper's ticket, he had a simple theory on what to do with it. George was a hard worker who believed in teaching other people. So he taught others how to drive and how to read the river. It was how he had learned and he said that was the way it should be done. He was one of the first captains for the tourist trade in Echuca aboard the *Canberra*. Several people from that era remember that George was a large part of making the *Canberra* a success not just as a tourist boat, but in making her 'warm'. George was known for his great sense of humour and would entertain passengers whenever he was out on the *Canberra*. George was an inventive captain and was always willing to take the *Canberra* out and hold different functions on her.

Known as a real 'old-time river character' George always wanted to be on the river. The water was something that pulled him in and the scent of steam was something that he had grown to know and love. In an interview at the age of seventy, George said: "There's something about the river that appeals."

George at the wheel of the *Canberra*.
Courtesy of Jennafer Whelan, George's daughter.

With money problems still plaguing the Echuca Syndicate, the time came to seriously consider leasing the boat to private businessmen. In March of 1970, the Syndicate leased the boat to Howard Bull, Ken Easdown and G. Adamson. The trio ran under the name Murray Steamship & Tourist Company. The Co-operative and those that were leasing the *Canberra* decided that running the steam engine was no longer fiscally viable and a diesel engine was sought. It was during this particular ownership that a diesel engine was installed on the *Canberra*. However, this particular conversion was beyond the fiscal capabilities of the Syndicate and Murray Steamship & Tourist Company. It was then that the Co-operative approached Echuca City Council for a loan. The arrangements for the loan worked well and the conversion to diesel was made.

The major condition of the loan agreement with the Council was that Murray Steamship & Tourist Company would have to upgrade the vessel's seating, interior as well as upgrading the PA system for the commentary. The Marshall steam engine was supposed to be cut up for scrap and removed but this never occurred. The pistons and flywheel were removed from the steam engine and a chain drive reconnected the engine to the paddle shaft. This gave the illusion that the steam engine was driving the wheels. The diesel, a Perkins marine engine with a velvet drive gearbox powered the paddlewheels via a worm drive reduction box. Many people were saddened by the demise of the steam engine but it led to the business becoming more viable financially.

Murray Steamship & Tourist Company maintained the lease for many years and 1980 saw them make a move to become more fiscally involved with the ownership of the *Canberra*, as they had been responsible for the maintenance and day to day running of the vessel. This caused problems with the Co-operative and they refused to allow Howard Bull, Ken Easdown and G. Adamson to purchase shares from lesser holders as it threatened their grip on the *Canberra*. It was also during this time that the *Pride of the Murray* started her tourism cruises. This caused some competition on the river and caused the Co-operative and Murray Steamship & Tourist Company some problems. With two boats now operating out of Echuca, there was less money being brought into the Co-operative. Numbers dropped and money was harder to find and the *Canberra's* future came into question about ownership and whether the leases should continue. This was compounded by the fact that in 1981, the main paddle shaft needed to be replaced and once again financial issues plagued the replacement.

1981 saw a captain by the name of Ted Lynne come aboard who would have some interesting times as skipper. The most notable of which included departing from the landing with the *Canberra* still attached! Ted had the Indian High Commissioner on board and was so excited he forgot to ask the hostess, Essie Nisbet, to release the lines. Another notable story was when Ted was taking the *Canberra* on a regular cruise and ran the vessel into a tree, causing massive damage in the process.

At the time of the accident in 1981, the Murray was in flood. During a turn, the skipper lost control of the vessel and the boat was caught in a cross current, slamming the *Canberra* into overhanging branches. The roof of the top deck collapsed and considerable damage was done to the port (left hand side) paddle box. Despite the slight mishaps, the 1980s were a time of great growth and prosperity for Echuca-Moama.

1985 saw the Murray Steamship & Tourist Company become very interested in purchasing the *Canberra*. The Syndicate asked for the *Canberra* to be evaluated by an independent source. After an agreement by both Murray Steamship & Tourist Company and the Co-operative, the *P.S. Canberra* was valued at $150,500 by P&O Australia. The purchase was finalised in 1985 by Murray Steamship & Tourist Company. After 19 years of operation by the Echuca Co-operative Syndicate, the *P.S. Canberra* returned to private ownership. The money earned by the Syndicate with the sale of the *P.S. Canberra* was reinvested into the Echuca–Moama area with the intention of continuing the tourism industry and further progress.

The damage done to the *Canberra* during the incident where Ted Lynne ran into a tree during a turn in high waters. Courtesy of Allan Bartsch and Neil Hutchinson.

Despite a year of low water in 1985 making travel trickier than usual, the *Canberra* still operated. The water was so low that Ted Lynne was photographed by the *Riverine Herald* knee deep in water halfway across the river. This was something most unusual for the Murray since the locks and weirs had been put in place.

Throughout the 1970s until the 1990s there were many skippers on the Murray River in and around Echuca who owed their skipper's tickets, at least in part, to the *Canberra*. Several stories from that era are still retold by skippers along the river.

Another of the skippers to grace the helm of the *Canberra* was Don Fraser. Known as a fill-in skipper for when other full time captains were away or ill, Don has his fair share of stories about the *Canberra* and the people that worked on her. One particular story involves the *Canberra* being sunk at her mooring. After large chunks of disused concrete had been dropped into the river near the *Canberra* mooring, the current dislodged a piece and shifted it under the hull. When returning to her mooring with George Vickers at the wheel, the concrete tore a hole in the hull "roughly the size of your fist" and filled the hull with water to the waterline. Once again the call went out for help. Don Fraser and Kevin Hutchinson were the ones who answered. Don had never fixed the hull of a boat in his life and was somewhat startled when he was told he had the job. Kevin looked over at Don and said: "Don't worry, the guys in NSW Maritime will tell you what to do over the phone." This was of small comfort to Don, nevertheless, he and Kevin did manage to patch up the boat.

The next day, George inspected the patch and invited Don on board. George said that they were going to take the *Canberra* out to test the patch job. Somewhat uncertain, Don mentioned that there were passengers coming on board.

George replied, "They can help test it too."

Startled by this, Don asked, "But what if she sinks?"

"Then she sinks," George replied with a smile. "Not like the bank is very far away."

Ted Lynne standing in the Murray River at Echuca. Courtesy of Essie Nisbet and the Riverine Herald.

Down to the waterline at her mooring after her hull was punctured.

During the era of skippers such as Don, there was one person who spent a great deal of her time on the water as a deckhand. Said to never have complained about her work and always delighting in meeting new people, Essie Nisbet is the longest serving deckhand of the *P.S. Canberra*. During her 20,360 trips aboard the *Canberra,* she had many experiences and worked under 30 different skippers. She speaks highly of them all saying that she didn't ever have a cross word to say to them. The number of stories that Essie has are beyond count. She was on board when Ted Lynne ran into trouble in the high waters, slamming the *Canberra* into trees, as well as the time he drove off with the landing still attached. One particular story includes a Christmas Cruise on the *P.S. Canberra*. Beforehand, gifts for the children that were cruising were stored on board so that Santa could hand out the presents. Everyone was aboard except for Santa who was nowhere to be seen. The captain waited as long as he could, but had to leave without Santa so the day's cruise schedule wasn't ruined. As *Canberra* passed the Echuca Wharf there was a loud thud on the top deck over the paddle box. Essie looked up from the bottom deck and saw Santa.

She stared at him and asked, "How'd you get there?"

Santa went on to explain that he had been running late and noticed the boat was leaving and so had run up to the wharf and jumped off.

Essie wasn't the only one in her family to work on the *Canberra*. Her son Rob also worked on board, as a cleaner. She recalls that she would go down with him to make sure he was doing a good job and would help him out on occasions. He made $1000 while working on board and promised his mother to spend it on something worthwhile because he had earned the money the hard way. Another of Essie's story involves Ted Lynne. They had been carrying stuff down onto the *Canberra* and loading up the kiosk on board when Essie heard Ted making an exasperated noise. She turned around and asked what had happened. Ted had dropped his glasses through the sponson decks. Not having much of a choice, the *Canberra* went out on her scheduled cruises for the day. At the end of the day, Essie and Ted decided to look for the lost glasses. Essie stood on the gangway whilst Ted waded into the water in nothing more than his briefs. He held onto the sponsons and felt around with his feet. The problem with the water around the *Canberra's* mooring, was that the bank was particularly muddy, so finding things there wasn't entirely an easy thing. Ted swung his feet through the water and up the side of the boat. One swing, he lifted his foot out of the water and his glasses were hooked over the top of his toes. Essie watched it happen and said it was something of a fluke.

A week later, a woman and her partner were coming down the gangway. Essie and Ted were helping the partner down the gangway as he was in a wheelchair. When they were all safely on board the *Canberra,* there was a noise of frustration. Essie turned to see the woman had dropped her keys in the water. Convincing her that they would look for the keys when they returned, the *Canberra* left and went on the cruise. On returning, Ted waded out into the water as he had done before. Much to everyone's surprise and to Essie's in particular, the keys were recovered in the same way as Ted had found his glasses.

One person who Essie worked with was Pearl Wallace, the first female skipper on the Murray River. Essie recalls that on several occasions, the passengers would look at the two of them and be a little worried. There was one man in particular who said he wasn't sure if he was going to go on the boat because the crew was two women. Essie supposed that the man's wife talked him into it and: "…by the end of the trip, he was thanking us."

Essie Nisbet

Essie alongside Pearl Wallace on
the *Canberra*. Circa 1977.
Courtesy of Essie Nisbet

Passengers being loaded onto the *Canberra* from the top
deck of the Kiosk at Riverboat Dock, 1973.
Courtesy of Heather Rendle and
the Echuca Historical Society

Those years, also saw the first appearance of a future skipper, Neil Hutchinson. At age twelve, whenever he would go on the *Canberra,* he remembers other skippers like Allan Bartsch and Andy Simpson would let him drive. In conversations with Neil, he often says that he would have spent as many hours behind the wheel of the *Canberra* unqualified as well as qualified. He says that he owes many hours to the *Canberra* for helping him gain his qualifications. It was his years of working on the *Canberra* that inspired him to push for the vessel to be returned to steam.

1979 saw the *Canberra* imprinted onto a 20c stamp for Australia Post. The stamps included other vessels, such as the *P.S. Murray River Queen* as part of the *Ferries and Steamers* series. This was a first for the Echuca paddle steamers and tourism trade. It would be several years before other vessels would make the post stamps.

The tourism industry boomed and the town grew. More vessels joined the *Canberra* on the river and hundreds of thousands of people became part of the multitudes of people that would travel along the Murray River. This trend continued well into the 1990s. It seemed that the Collins brothers' dream of the *Canberra* being a successful tourist vessel had indeed been realised, just in the wrong city. In their later years, the Collins brothers and Arch Conner returned to enjoy journeys on the *P.S. Canberra*, although as passengers.

P.S. Canberra alongside the *P.S. Adelaide* before the dry dock levee bank broke, Feb 1993

P.S. Canberra at Echuca Wharf, late 1960s.
Courtesy of Murray River Paddlesteamers

Dec 1974

P.S. Canberra at her mooring, 1974.
Courtesy of Pete Garfield.

P.S. Canberra in Mildura, 1963.
Courtesy of Kevin Hutchinson

P.S. Canberra during the rebuild of 2002 and 2003.
Courtesy of Murray River Paddlesteamers

P.S. Canberra during the rebuild of 2002 and 2003.
Courtesy of Murray River Paddlesteamers

More repairs to the *P.S. Canberra*.

In Lock 26 at Torrumbarry

EDNA
2QN
DIAL 1520 FOR THE SOUND THE
...SES

Courtesy of James McDougall

P.S. Canberra at Echuca, 2013.
By James McDougall

S.S. CANBERRA
ECHUCA
James McDougall 2012

Courtesy of Al and Kylie Tracey

June 1987 saw ownership of the *Canberra* transfer to Marie and Clive Pilley and Janice and Tod Collins. The management was under the watchful eye of Len Nigro. During the first few years of ownership, the two families worked hard to restore parts of the *Canberra* that needed attention. Allan Bartsch became the main full time skipper, who also helped with the upkeep of vessel. 'Bartschy' spoke of his time aboard the *Canberra* saying that he had fun. "There were no troubles or politics. If there was, I did my best to stay out of it. Working with Essie was good. She was always there, with a cup of coffee for the skipper followed by some fruit cake. She never complained about it ever. She loved it. Clive and Tod were brilliant to work with. Nothing was too hard for them and they were obliging as boat owners, happy to fix anything that needed fixing. Best of all, they were just great to chat to. They listened to what we had to say. The *Canny* was the boat that was there to be worked on when I started. When I did start, I worked mostly with Ted Lynne and Andy Simpson."

Clive and Tod continued to run the *Canberra* as she had been run since her arrival in Echuca. They were particularly successful as it was a time when there were no poker machines in Victoria. Great busloads of tourists from Melbourne, generally older people, would come to Echuca for the weekend. The bus groups would book trips on the *Canberra,* then would venture over to Moama and spend money. It was a boom period for the *Canberra* and indeed Echuca–Moama

On February 26, 1993, the *Canberra* escaped serious damage after the dry dock near the wharf in Echuca was flooded and the levee bank broke. The sandbags that had been holding back the water gave way and flooded the area with about two metres of water. The force of the water threw the *Canberra* into the river where she crashed into the *P.S. Adelaide.* Skipper Andy Simpson was asleep on the top deck when the levee bank broke. There was only minor damage to the *Canberra.* Simpson was quoted as saying that if the accident had happened the previous day when men had been working under the vessel, it would have killed them. The cost to fix the vessel and the levee would be $20,000 to co-owners, Tod Collins and Clive Pilley.

A flood in 1993 saw those that worked on the *P.S. Canberra* and along the Murray and its tributaries adjust to waters and conditions that hadn't been seen since 1974. The gangway of the *Canberra's* landing had to be lengthened by a good 30 metres so that passengers were able to board the vessel. Unlike the high waters of 2012 the skippers, vessels and crew of 1993 continued to operate and carry passengers. When the *Canberra* and vessels like her were built they were designed at a time when the river wasn't controlled by the locks and weirs that were put in as a result of the 1914–1915 drought. The *Canberra* in particular was designed to be easy to manoeuvre and manage shallower waters than larger vessels. Like all vessels of that time, the *Canberra* has a flat bottomed hull, to make a shallower draft as river vessels aren't subject to a tidal water flow. The 1993 floods saw torn down trees and all manner of debris coming down the river. The vessels then operating on the Murray River at Echuca navigated the water as they had always done. In Echuca at the current time of writing, there is a kiosk that used to support the local swimming pool when the pool itself was in the river – not an unusual occurrence for the time. The water of the 1993 floods completely flooded the lower level of the building.

December 1994 saw a very windy day where the boats were all having trouble traversing the water. Larger vessels, such as the *P.S. Pevensey* and the *P.S. Emmylou* hadn't left their moorings, nor would it have been prudent to do so. However, the *Canberra,* being smaller and more manoeuverable was taken out. Lance Bramley, who was skipper that day, decided to try his luck heading downstream. This turned out to be something of a problem. The wind whipped up under the promenade deck and peeled it back. Whilst this was going on, there was a gentleman who insisted that Lance turn the *Canberra* around so he could retrieve his hat, which had blown off! Struggling against the wind and to return to mooring, the hat was left behind. The call went out for help and as usual, the boating community responded. The roof was reattached and the *Canberra* was fixed and able to be used again the next day.

In 1995, a letter from David Fitton, a skipper of the *Canberra* saw the first official whispers of returning the *Canberra* to steam driven. Before that letter, previous skippers, including Andy 'Sandbar' Simpson had already started the process of restoring the engine. Sandbar was one of the first to return the engine to working order, mostly for use as a heater. In time, the engine parts started moving and steaming. This created the sights and smells of a real paddle steamer. In interviews with Sandbar during the restoration process, he said, "People always comment how original the boat is and this is happening more and more now that the engine is steaming, even though at reduced pressure." Sandbar said, "…it would be a tragedy if such a unique piece of Australiana is not recognised and preserved."

This restoration work continued with the manager of the vessel, Len Nigro. He, along with other captains sought out a grant to return the *Canberra* to being a steamer. With many people, including factions at the Port of Echuca and private citizens contributing to the submission for the grant, it seemed possible that the *Canberra* would be returned to her former self. Unfortunately, at the time the push was unsuccessful. The denial came in late 2000 and the *Canberra* remained a diesel for the time being. A year later, the *Canberra* was sold to Max Vulling to have alongside his two other vessels, the *P.S. Emmylou* and the *Pride of the Murray*.

Max Vulling

Current owners of the *P.S. Canberra*, Max and Nola Vulling, have owned her since December of 2001.

"My knowledge with the history of the *Canberra* is limited compared to the staff. I'd been in Echuca for five years when we got the *Canberra*. What I learned about her and the other people who worked and had her is mainly from the locals and staff. I'm aware of the unique stature of the *Canberra* and that she was the original boat, or at least mostly. The foresight of the locals that brought her up here allowed her to start the tourist trade in Echuca. Seventeen or eighteen years later the movie 'All the Rivers Run' really put Echuca on the tourist map, but *Canberra* was the first. She was the one that started it all.

Max Vulling

"Turning her back to steam was a big undertaking, it was the staff though that really pushed for it. That made the *Canberra* special too, turning her back to steam was really unusual. She's the only one gone from steam to diesel and then back to steam.

"The *Canberra* had been on the radar to buy for quite a while. The *Pride of the Murray* came first, then the *Emmylou*. The *Canberra* was the last one left at River Boat Dock. We bought her because of her history and her position at the dock was logical to have. All three boats could do similar things but are very different in feel. The *Canberra* is the ideal boat for families and kids. She's the only one that you can see practically all of the engine and drive the boat as well. There was no real reason to turn the *Canberra* back to steam, but I asked the guys, 'are you behind it?' and they were. It was supposed to be three months of a rebuild and it became nine months. But it was worth it in the end. Over time, she's becoming popular once again. Parents are bringing their kids back because they remember the *Canberra* from when they were kids.

In late 2002 and early 2003, Max Vulling undertook the challenge to rebuild the *Canberra*. The boat was winched backwards up the Moama slipway in September 2002 and the lower deck cabins and main deck were quickly dismantled. The diesel engine and gearbox were removed and the once working vessel quickly took on the appearance of a wreck. At one stage the roof and promenade deck were propped up only by a few slender poles and it was feared a strong wind could collapse the lot. Major repairs were carried out on the hull including reframing the entire engine room and placing new steel floor beams to support the steam engine. The main and sponson decks were re-framed, a new rudder and the paddle boxes were rebuilt. Slowly some strength returned to the structure. A new main deck was laid, using Oregon timber recycled from 100 year old beams. She was also given 17 new red gum planks and most of the keelson and ribs in the hull were replaced. Neil Hutchinson, Andrew Cook, Jeff Robertson, Gary Aitken, Ben Klaster, Hume Colville, Phil Morton, Peter Garfield and Phil Cadell were the major crew behind the renovations, with many more helping out along the way.

Picture shows some of the crew positioning the chimney stack on the new steam engine.

The major push behind returning the *Canberra* to steam was from Neil Hutchinson. Having been around boats and steam all his life, Neil wanted to see the long serving *Canberra* returned to steam and with help from an enthusiastic crew this eventuated. The surveyor sent from Sydney by the NSW Maritime Authority quickly poured cold water on Neil's dream though. After a cursory inspection the surveyor was not impressed with the condition of the original boiler and would not allow its return to operation without more extensive repairs. A later inspection by a land based boiler inspector overturned the marine engineer's report. With the help of Kevin Hutchinson and other members of the steam world another engine was sourced and used to replace the original engine. This engine too required more repairs than was first anticipated. The boat was repainted and the stark white cabins were replaced by a more muted tone. The trim colour was changed again to royal blue and gold to reflect the boat's connection with the city she was named after. Despite being red and white for most of her career *Canberra's* trim had changed colour a number of times: blue in 1969 and green in 1975. It was during this time of repainting that the paddles themselves were lowered into the water. During the reconstruction there were many different companies that assisted the rebuild team. Once the major work was completed on the slipway, the *Canberra* was returned to the water and floated over to her mooring on the Victorian bank.

Neil Hutchinson

Born July 20, 1973

Part of the following is written by Neil about his time aboard the *P.S. Canberra* and the restoration work that he took part in:

"One of the funniest things happened after we had her (the *Canberra*) in steam. We had a 5 chime loco whistle on her and we gave it a good hoot whilst tied up at River Boat Dock. Well, this kid came flying through the engine room screaming 'We're gunna die' and took off up the gangway.

"The *Canberra* has always been a constant in my life. Ironically, I had my masters ticket for 9 years before I finally got to take her out by myself. I would nearly say I have done as many miles behind the wheel unqualified. It was always a good way to kill time as a kid — go for a couple of trips on the *Canny*. Andy (Simpson) and Bartschy (Allan Bartsch) were always willing to give you a go. As I got older I got the job to go on the charters. Some of those were pretty wild in their day. I also had the job of cleaner and hit the big time then, $70 a week, not bad money for a 16 year old.

When I was 20 I spent about 9 months working on her for nothing to realise my ticket. Lots of people owe something to the *Canberra* in terms of using it for getting time up. I think that was a driving factor in wanting to give something back when it came to fixing her up. We all put in some pretty big days and nights to achieve it. The restoration of the *Canberra* prior to this was most probably in a bit of peril. Each time the surveyors turned up they were less impressed by her condition. One of her biggest problems was the timber sheer plank that most of the boat above the water sits on. That is why we had to deconstruct her to the extent we did in order to get her back to something you could work with."

Neil hard at work after the completion
of the front deck of the *P.S. Canberra*.
Courtesy of Murray River Paddlesteamers.

Neil was brought up with the history of the boats. His father, Kevin, would take him down to the boats and Andy Simpson, a captain of the *Canberra* at the time, lived around the corner from the Hutchinson family and would also take Neil with him.

Neil considers the *Canberra* to be something of a survivor and that she was the start of the tourism trade as she was only boat in Echuca before *The Pride of the Murray* was commissioned. "Lots of blokes from the 70s and 80s owe their tickets to the *Canberra*.

"The kiosk out the back had louvre windows that the possums would open and get into the shop. While there, the possums would make a big mess and leak over the stuff in the kiosk." Neil remembers as a kid the *Canberra* was a good source of money because there was a hole in the deck and people would accidently drop their money down the hole. Neil was also bribed by Essie at times to carry stuff down to the boat and would be rewarded by a lolly.

"One of the things you will see when people come on the *Canberra* is their reaction when they are confronted by the engine at eye level: the polished brass, the wheel and the sort, the reaction is usually: *Wow!* It is one of those atmospheres that you will not find on any other boat."

2002 saw the eve of the *Canberra's* 90th birthday and she was taken out of the water for a complete restoration.
It was during this time that she was returned to having a fully operational steamer, rather than being diesel powered.
Courtesy of Murray River Paddlesteamers.

Neil hopes that the *Canny* continues on as she is, because she is an important part of Echuca and the tourism trade. He stresses the great importance she has had and that she has been an unusual boat that has brought many different people together. He says, "I have a soft spot for her, I suppose."

P.S. Canberra being returned to the water after being stripped. The cabin and interior were replaced on the Victorian bank at berth four at River Boat Dock. Courtesy of Murray River Paddlesteamers.

With the *Canberra* on the Victorian side of the Murray, repairs continued and her cabin was restored. The fore and aft decks were opened up so that passengers were able to sit outside the vessel, rather than being confined to the inside of the lower deck. The top deck was given more secure enclosures and fitted with permanent seating, rather than removable seating. The interior was replaced with baltic pine that created a warmer atmosphere. Max Vulling, the owner, said that in restoring the *P.S. Canberra* it would ensure that she would remain as: "A prominent feature in Echuca-Moama's river history."

The project to return the *Canberra* to steam and redo her interior took nine months to complete.

It wasn't until June in 2003 that the *Canberra* was officially relaunched. Her major crew for the first trip being Captain Neil Hutchinson and engineer Peter Garfield. The ceremony, celebrating both the *Canberra's* 90th birthday and the restoration was opened by Essie Nisbet, the longest serving deckhand on the *P.S. Canberra*. Vessels from Echuca sailed past the *Canberra* and a blast of whistles greeted the *Canberra* back to official work. She is still the most continuously used vessel on the river. The opening was attended by many different people before the official first cruise. This cruise entailed members of the community who were invited aboard to see how the *P.S. Canberra* had been refurbished. This select group included members of the Echuca Syndicate, members of the Echuca-Moama community, and further afield those who had served both previously and currently aboard the vessel. After that official cruise, the general public were invited aboard. The day went off without a hitch and the *Canberra* was once again a true paddle steamer of Echuca.

Once recommissioned, the *Canberra* and her crew undertook some adventurous journeys. Some of these included trips through Lock 26, at Torrumbarry Weir. The first of these occurring during July of 2003. The day cruises were conducted as usual then afterwards, the engine room was loaded full of firewood and provisions and set off for the afternoon. One particular trip the

The *P.S. Canberra* at Torrumbarry Weir, 2003
Courtesy of Murray River Paddlesteamers.

boat pulled up at around midnight. The group had a quick beer, then were off to bed. Some of the women from the office at Murray River Paddlesteamers had come along for the trip. When the swags were being rolled out there were squeals and a mad panic. The swag was filled with cockroaches and there was a scramble to kill them before they invaded the boat.

During her years with Murray River Paddlesteamers, the *Canberra* travelled to places she had never been previously, one place being Barmah.

On departure from Barmah, the *P.S. Emmylou* took off in front of the *Canberra*. Unfortunately, the crew of the *Emmylou* didn't have enough steam pressure in the boiler, so the late Paul Herman, skipper at the time, told the crew of the *Canberra* to come around as the

The maiden voyage of the relaunched *Canberra* at Echuca over the Queens' Birthday long weekend, 9th June, 2003 for her 90th birthday.
Courtesy of Murray River Paddlesteamers

Canberra was already up to pressure. As the *Canberra* went past the *Emmylou* the crew thought of an interesting prank to play. They decided that it would make for some good photos if they stuck a whole car tyre on the fire to make her billow great black smoke everywhere. And as a bonus, the smoke would generally annoy Paul, the skipper. A tyre was brought down into the engine room and hog tied to make it bow in the middle. The engineer shoved the tyre through the door of the firebox. The desired effect was achieved with great black smoke billowing from the stack of the *Canberra,* blocking out the whole river behind the boat and the captain on the *Emmylou* yelling abuse through the UHF radio.

P.S. Canberra and *P.S. Emmylou* tied together at Cape Horn Winery in 2003.
Courtesy of Murray River Paddlesteamers

Peter Garfield

Born December 11, 1963

Pete is a current skipper and engineer for the *P.S. Canberra*. He grew up in Canberra city and his love of the river and paddle steamers comes from spending his school holidays in the town of Boundary Bend. His grandmother showed him some history books and snapshots of the *P.S. Etona* and *P.S. Hero* taken in the 1950s. Whilst in Boundary Bend his grandfather would take him out in his tinny, past the wreck of the *P.S. Hero*, to check his illegal drum nets. Pete started his career as a volunteer on the *P.S. Enterprise* on Lake Burley Griffin in Canberra in 1989. He moved to Echuca in early 1997 to be engine driver on *P.S. Emmylou* and gained his Masters ticket in 1998. He spent many hours repainting the *Canberra* during the restoration in 2002-03. Pete has spent the last 11 years and estimated 13000 trips working on the *P.S. Canberra*.

Peter holding the certificate for the *Canberra's* inclusion on the registrar of Historical Vessels.
Courtesy of the Riverine Herald.

Peter is also a great lover of history. In particular, he has focused on the history of the *Canberra*. Over the years he has collected stories about her, the river and the families of the area. He liked the *Canberra* because she was a smaller vessal, had history and had been converted back to steam, which was unprecedented on the Murray. For Pete, it was exciting to work on an historical vessel. "Norm Collins taking the camping and fishing cruises in 1944 is one of the most interesting things I've learned about the *Canberra's* history. The roads were terrible back then and there were places you could only get to by boat.

"Lots of interesting things have happened on the *Canberra*. Doing the morning cruises up to Echuca village was fun. You'd leave really early, before sunrise in winter, to get there in time. The peace and tranquillity of the river was lovely. Often the deckhand would cook breakfast for us. We'd pick up the kids who were on holidays and take them back to Echuca so they'd do trips around the port. Taking *Canberra* through the lock at Torrumbarry was fun.

"During the rebuild, in early 2003 when the boat was back in the river, Phil Cadel was using an angle grinder in the galley when his pants caught fire from the sparks.

We started calling out to him: "Phil you're on fire!" but he couldn't hear us over the noise of the grinder.

"Whaaaa?" was the reply. He was surrounded by tins of paint and brushes soaking in turps.

"PHIL YOU'RE ON FIRE!" we yelled again.

Finally, the penny dropped and Phil ran around beating out the flames swearing loudly. That was an interesting day."

Having worked on the *Canberra* for some time, Pete has a great affinity with her. One of the things that he most enjoys about the boat is its great atmosphere on board.

"The ability to be working on the same level as the deckhand and the engineer is something that makes the day better. There's no one higher than the other and everyone is equal."

For the future of the *Canberra,* Peter would like to see: "…the original engine put back in to the *Canny*. Be nice to reunite the two parts of her."

Celebrating the *P.S. Canberra's* forty years of service in Echuca.
Essie Nisbet and Pete Garfield, 16 January 2006.
Courtesy of the Riverine Herald

P.S. Canberra in Echuca.
Courtesy of Murray River Paddlesteamers

Murray River Paddlesteamers were great innovators for unusual trips, due in no small part to the operators, Max Vulling and Vern Beasley. Often they had trips for charity organisations such as the Country Fire Authority. One particular trip in 2004 saw the *Canberra* used as a relief craft for when the CFA members would return from various leadership and team building exercises. The *Canberra* was loaded up with mountain bikes, canoes and tents and was used as the logistics base for two days. The *Canberra* would steam to a location, drop the CFA crew off then head to the next location. Journeys like this were not unusual. Quite often, the trips aboard the *Canberra* were purely for the entertainment of the crew, who after all, "are a little bit mad and like sniffing on steam."

In 2006, the *P.S. Canberra* celebrated 40 years of service in Echuca. By this time Essie Nisbet had done 20,360 trips on the *P.S. Canberra*, spanning a 30 year career aboard the vessel. In an interview with the *Riverine Herald,* Essie spoke of her fondness for the *P.S. Canberra* and the time she had spent aboard the boat. She recounted stories of her time aboard over her long career including when she met Princess Diana and Prince Charles during their 1985 visit. Essie said that was an "unreal moment" for her but it was a moment that would stay with her for the rest of her life.

With a push from the owner, the crew and members of the community, proceedings for the *P.S. Canberra* to be considered an historic part of Australia and the Murray River began. This took quite some time and in the year 2010 the *Canberra* was officially registered on the Australian Register of Historic Vessels. By being added to the list, the *Canberra* is among some of the most famous vessels in Australian History. Peter Garfield said that the inclusion of the *Canberra* on the list was an acknowledgement of the contribution that the *Canberra* had made to the tourism industry, especially in Echuca. At the time she was added to the list, she had been operating continuously for 45 years. The *Canberra* is arguably, the longest serving tourist vessel on the Murray River. The inclusion of the *Canberra* to the Historic Vessels means that her future is set and the vessel will continue to operate for many years to come.

Max and Nola Vulling have owned the *P.S. Canberra* since December of 2001. They have since leased the vessel to MRPS whose dedicated team continue to run the *P.S. Canberra* and two other vessels on the Murray River, running out of River Boat Dock. This was the first mooring of the *P.S. Canberra* and the original site of Henry Hopwood's (the founder of Echuca) punt crossing across the Murray River. The history of the *Canberra* is something that has always been known among the river people, but never fully explored. From her humble beginnings as a fishing and light cargo vessel, owned by savvy businessman, David Conner, as part of a successful fishing fleet; to the first vessel to be used for tourists vessel by the Collins brothers; to being brought to Echuca by a group of businessmen; to serving the community of Echuca for over 40 years. The *P.S. Canberra* is embedded in the history of Australia and the legend of the Murray-Darling Basin. She is one of the longest continuously used working treasures on the Murray River.

List of Captains and Engineers of the PS Canberra while a Tourist Vessel

---

Allan Bartsch	Bill Hogg	Dave Sorensen
Lance Bramley	Hillary (Paddy) Hogg	Vern Stack
Tony Brown	Kevin Hutchinson	P W Symons
Max Carrington Snr	Neil Hutchinson	Les Telley
Max Carrington Jnr	Clare Jackson	Andrew Talbot
Andrew Cook	Malcom Lowe	Damien Taylor
Bill Collins	Ted Lynne	Don Taylor
Norm Collins	Darren Mann	Bob Trapnell
Lyle Flack	George Marsh	Graeme Trist
David Fitton	Peter McLeod	Hamish Turner
Kathy Forte	James McDougall	Bill Vickers
Don Fraser	Naomi Parker	George Vickers
George Buck Freeman	Beresford Ralph	Paul Vickers
Peter Garfield	Andy 'Sandbar' Simpson	Pearl Wallace
Eddie Hazelman	Denise Simpson	Jenny Watson
Paul Herman		Dick Wrangles

Engineers
without masters' tickets

Gary Aitken

Jeff Leverett

Darren Morgan

Phil Morton

Warwick Turner

The PS Canberra

Launched: August 2, 1913

Measurements: 22.55 metres

Moulded Breadth: 4.50 metres

Moulded Depth: 1.20 metres

Weight: 51 tonne

Crew: 3

Max passengers: 99 passengers

Total of 102 people on board

Hull material: wood

Identifying number: 17634

The Original Steam Engine

With the *Canberra's* original engine, David wanted it to be fast and rival his brother's vessel the *Etona*. As this was the case, he ordered the engine especially. Part of the special order was silent chain or Reynolds chain, the same as the *Etona,* a larger firebox and reversing motion. Although the original steamer was constructed as a semi-portable, it was actually ordered for the boat. The engine was sent to: David Conner c/– steamer *Fairy,* Mildura. Although addressed to Mildura the engine was more likely to have gone straight to Goolwa where the hull of the *Canberra* was. At the time the engine was made the makers of the boiler, Marshall and Sons, had made over 193,000 engines, boilers and thrashing machines among other styles of engines. Of all the steamers in preservation, six of them boast Marshall engines. The original engine dimensions are 8 inch bore, 12 inch stroke, Stephensons link reversing motion with a 100 psi operating pressure. The engine is unusual in another way as it is without the usual Marshall name castings. The reason for this is unknown, though it would possibly make the engine cheaper to initially purchase.

The original engine with a flywheel.
Order N: 402, Jan 8 1913
Engine: No.61299
Card No: P131
Double Cylinder, Special firebox, silent driving chain
Delivered by: *SS Port Augusta* 33, direct to Adelaide
Date landed: July 25, 1913, deferred duty paid Adelaide wharf
Cost: 426 pounds two shillings, one penny
Sold to: JD Conner, Address *Fairy*. Mildura
Date Sold: July 22,1913
Net Sale Price: £525
Percentage profit: 24 ¼ percent
Extract from Robison & Bros & Co Melbourne, agents for
Marshall Sons & Co order book 1901 to 1930

With the original engine in the foreground, the new engine is
being lowered into the *Canberra*. Early 2003.
Courtesy of Peter Garfield.

The registration number on an original piece of timber
from 1913. Taken 7 March, 2013 by Peter Garfield.

The Second Steam Engine

The second of the steam engines that has powered the *Canberra* is a 1923 Marshall and Sons, portable steam engine, imported for the McDonald family of Murrabit to power a water pump on their property. The Marshall was sourced by Neil and Kevin Hutchinson after the original engine was deemed unusable. Engine repairs were undertaken at the workshops of Hume Colville at Barham where Neil Hutchinson and Dave Sorensen installed a new set of boiler tubes. The engine was rebuilt, reversing gear fabricated and the chain drives installed by Ben Klaster and Gary Aitken. The engine was installed in January 2003 where Phil Morton began fabricating the miles of pipework needed to make the engine operational.

Class: C F L Portable Steam Engine
Order No: 487
Date: Oct 26, 1923
Engine No: 77069 Card No. P199
Delivery Ship: S.S. Hobsons Bay
Date landed: Jan 7, 1924
Cost: £876 twelve shillings and eleven pence
Buyer: Mr. C.H. McDonald, **Riversdale**, Myall, via Kerang
Date Sold: Jan 29, 1924
Net Sale Price: £985
Profit percentage: 12 1/3 percent

P..S. Canberra at Echuca Wharf, late 1960s.
Courtesy of Murray River Paddlesteamers

During her running life as a diesel, the *Canberra* also wore out two Perkins engines in the 30 years of having them, the third only being taken out for conversion. The last remnants of the *Canberra's* life as a diesel engine is an electric horn that was kept on the front of the boat as a nod to her years of being run by the Perkins engines. There are parts of the *Canberra* that are also still the original boat. Several beams along her roofline to the upper deck as well as sections of the engine room have been kept as part of her original structure.

One of the greatest attributes of the *Canberra* is her atmosphere. It has been said by many passengers that it is great to see the crew working so closely together and having fun doing so. Another unusual thing about her is that her engine is at eye level and close to the observer. From one particular trip, a passenger was asked to describe the boat and what she thought of the *Canberra*. Her response was simply the word: "shiny".

From the perspective of the 'steam boffins' and 'boating fruit loops' and other people who have worked on her, the *Canberra* is a place to catch up. Everyone can sit around, have a chat and relax. In earlier days, when disagreements arose between companies, the *Canberra* was considered neutral territory, where everyone was welcome to discuss anything. In many ways, the *Canberra* still holds that title. To be able to stand around and chat to co-workers as well as the people who work on the river on other vessels is something that is still done. It is a community. The community of the Riverboat People in Echuca was reignited by the *P.S. Canberra*. It was she who started the tourism trade that reminded generations that the Murray River and paddle steamers are an integral and important part of the history of Australia.

Someone once said about paddle steamers: "…that a bit of the smoke gets into your lungs and a bit of the water into your blood and you're hooked for life." On August 2, 2013, the *P.S. Canberra* celebrated her centenary. She is loved by thousands and remembered by more. For those who work on her, it is a love and passion that brings them back for more. For those who look on from afar, it is a passion for not only the river, but these living, breathing creatures that allowed inland Australia to be opened up to travel and farming. The *P.S. Canberra* is a reminder of all that was and is on the river that is the Mighty Murray.

A Note from the Author:

My love affair of paddle steamers started when I was five years old. My grandfather took me out on the *P.S. Etona,* a boat that had once belonged to the family. It was on this trip that I first drove a boat. I'd been watching with great interest and learning all morning, when my grandfather Dave had looked over at me and asked if I wanted a drive. I nodded, wanting to experience something new. He picked me up and put me on a stool, my hands on the wheel. He asked, "Have you got it?"

Again, I nodded.

He then said, "Good, I'm off for a sleep." And then left the wheelhouse.

A few minutes later, my father came up to see me and asked where Grandpa was. I told my dad that he'd gone for a sleep. My father nodded, then stood in the doorway and watched me as I drove down the river. Thinking back, I'm not completely certain Grandpa left me on my own, but for a moment there, I felt like I was the skipper. It was that moment that started a love of the river and paddle steamers that will always be with me. I grew up on the Murray River in Boundary Bend, wanting to learn everything I could about the river and the boats that had worked on the reaches. Every chance I had to go on a paddle steamer, regardless of the name, I'd take. Even now, at the age of 23, I step onto a paddle steamer and feel like a small child again. The smell, the feel and the stories still fill me with enthusiasm.

Beth Conner

The *P.S. Canberra* has been part of my life for as long as I can remember. The *Canny*, having been built for my family, was always in stories and in photo frames on the walls of the homestead built by the Conner brothers, David (my great-grand uncle) and Arch (my great-grandfather). When I was younger, I'd fall asleep looking up at a framed photo of the *Canberra* above the door. The very first photo used in this book is the photo I would look at. That photo is still above the door at the place that is now called Conner Park. It would have been impossible to write this book without my family, whom I hold very dear. The *Canberra* is particularly special to me because of the 'feel' of her. The atmosphere is close and interesting: the chop of the paddlewheels as they churn through the water; the pull of the steering wheel against the current; the steam wafting through the sponsons; the scent of steam that seems to stick to the inside of your nose and will forever be familiar. To know that all her life, the *Canberra* has worked, regardless of the industry. It is especially nice to hold the wheel and know the history behind that wheel. It is with great love that I pay homage to the Conner family and all of the descendants, past and present.

It also has to be said that it would be impossible to have written this without my friends. Peter Garfield, Neil Hutchinson, James McDougall, Essie Nisbet, Warwick Turner, Eileen Bowen, Courtney Baty and Vern Beasley have been instrumental in writing this. Their support and knowledge has been greatly appreciated and valued. They have been there for me with information, encouragement and the occasional reminder to sleep. In particular, Pete who started the whole process and did a lot of research with me as well as sourcing hundreds of photos. Neil who made the process funny and reminded me that steam boffins are great value as well as smart. Courtney who kept me on track. Essie and Eileen who told me stories I'd never heard. And James who put up with my ranting and allowed me to stay when I needed to.

I'd also like to thank various people in the community who have helped create this book, filling the pages with stories and information from their days aboard the *Canberra*. Just some of these people include Don Oberin, Don Fraser, Kevin Hutchinson and Max Vulling. There are many whom have contributed to the words of this book and to all those, I thank you all.

My sister Sam and I on our first ever trip on a paddle steamer, *P.S. Etona*. Coming into Curlwaa at the Abbotsford Bridge 1995. I'm on the right.
Courtesy of Tim Conner

With Thanks:

Murray River Paddlesteamers, Vern and Julienne Beasley and their staff, thank you for giving me the opportunity to tell the story of the *P.S. Canberra*. Also for looking after me during the hours I've spent writing and researching.

The Riverine Herald

The Echuca Historical Society

Heather Rendle

The Sunraysia Daily

The Swan Hill Pioneer Settlement

The Swan Hill Guardian

Trove

State Library of South Australia

State Library of Victoria

National Library of Australia

Australian Defence Force Archives

Billy Hogg

Brian Flanagan

Murray Darling Basin Authority

Nancy Mason

Tony Newton

Jennafer Whelan

The owners, skippers, engineers and deckhands who have worked on and kept the *Canberra* over the course of her lifetime.

Personal thanks to the Family, the Countess, the Advisor and the Muse.

Beth Conner, 2013

Aug 1973, PS *Canberra* at her mooring.

David Conner

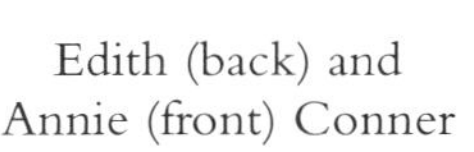

Edith (back) and
Annie (front) Conner

Wilie Conner (Jnr)

Lucy Conner

Sarah Conner

Arch Conner

Alic Conner

P.S. Canberra and *P.S. Etona*.
The Conner family are on the front of the *Etona*. 1924

P.S. Ranger being held up the bank by the *P.S. Canberra* and
the *P.S. Etona*. *P.S. Ranger* was punctured by a log and
Arch drove her up the bank. 1916

Part of the mosquito fleet of the Conner family. 1911

P.S. Canberra at Hay. 1917

P.S. Canberra in Mildura Lock, circa 1961.

P.S. Canberra in Mildura during the early sixties.

P.S. Canberra in Mildura, 1966.
Courtesy of Kevin Hutchinson

P.S. Canberra in Echuca.

Aug 1973, George Vickers walking
through the water.

P.S. Canberra while being run by Norm
and Bill Collins. During this time,
she was renamed the Showboat *Canberra*.
This photo comes from the early 1960s.
Courtesy of Murray Darling Basin Authority

Captain Andy Simpson looking after
the *Canberra's* engine. 1991

Paddle Steamers of Australia

P.S. Canberra - The First Hundred Years

Beth Conner with Captain Peter Garfield

ISBN 9781922175168   Qty

RRP   AU$29.99   .....

Postage within Australia   AU$5.00   .....

TOTAL★ $________

★ All prices include GST

Name:...

Address: ....

....

Phone:...

Email: ....

Payment: ❏ Money Order ❏ Cheque ❏ MasterCard ❏Visa

Cardholders Name:...

Credit Card Number: ....

Signature:...

Expiry Date: ....

Allow 7 days for delivery.

Payment to: Marzocco Consultancy (ABN 14 067 257 390)
                     PO Box 12544
                     A'Beckett Street, Melbourne, 8006
                     Victoria, Australia
                     admin@brolgapublishing.com.au